The Writer's Guide to Agony and Defeat

THE 43 WORST MOMENTS IN THE WRITING LIFE AND HOW TO GET OVER THEM

Jennie Nash

Interior Design by Jade Eby

For information on special sales and speaking engagements, contact the author at www.jennienash.com.

The Writer's Guide to Agony and Defeat/ Jennie Nash -- 1st ed.

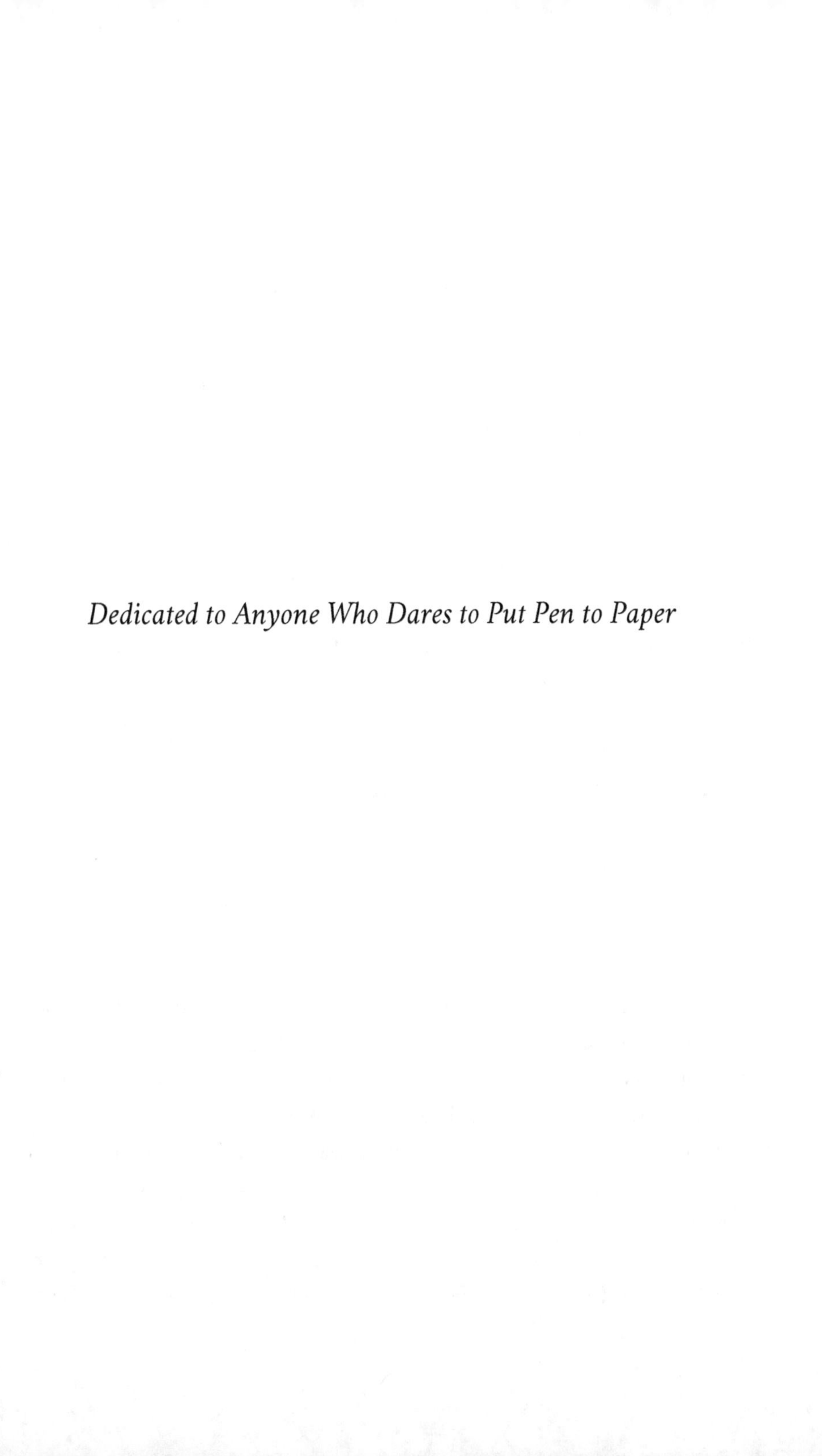

Dedicated to Anyone Who Dares to Put Pen to Paper

Introduction

WRITING A BOOK is like childbirth: no one ever tells you exactly how painful the process is going to be, and when you are in the middle of hurting you wonder if you are, perhaps, the only person in the history of the world who has ever felt exactly this awful. I've been a writer for 25 years, and a writing instructor and private book coach for seven, and I have either witnessed or experienced every possible kind of writerly pain. The possibilities for agony and defeat are everywhere — at the start of the process when a book idea is forming in your mind and doubt is pounding on the door; in the middle of the process when you begin to show your words to the world and fear gnaws at you like a disease; and at the end of the process when you hope your work will find an adoring audience and must come face to face with how much greed and envy have taken up residence in your heart. It can be a brutal business — but like childbirth, the deep satisfactions on the "pro" side tend to outweigh the long list of "cons," and so we forge ahead, writing our stories and often suffering our heartache.

I recently endured a seventh-month wait for my seventh book to find a publishing home. Every day my novel failed to sell, I imagined that my writing career — this thing I had nurtured since fourth grade and that I thought had grown unshakably strong — was coming to a quiet, bitter, wretched end. I'd had a good run, but it was over. I thought I might never get to write again. When friends would ask how things were going, I would shake my head and say, "Not well." But people don't empathize with a writer's private agonies — it's not like it's cancer or global financial meltdown — and they would quickly move on to talk about the latest Bourne movie or the beautiful heirloom tomatoes they got at the farmers' market. This made me even sadder, because now instead of just feeling like a tortured artist, I felt tortured and ridiculous. I had, after all, *chosen* to be a writer.

The enlightenment gurus say that you should "feel what you feel" so I began to wallow even deeper into my misery. I began to catalog the specific agonies of the writing life. I came up with 43. I figured I could turn my pain into something useful for my fellow writers who might feel less bleak about writing when they recognize their own particular moment of wretchedness set down on the page. I thought we could all feel a little less alone.

My story did not have a happy ending. My seventh book did not sell. I have published six books with major New York houses but book number seven turned out not to be so lucky. The irony is that it is far and away the best book I have written. The first six books helped me get to the place where I could write a much better book, but their less-than-blockbuster track record hamstrung me. I'm a midlist writer with modest sales numbers, and so now I am a writer with a book that has no home. Yes, I know, there is self publishing, and that will be happening. It's a good time to be a writer because there are so many more opportunities available to us than there were in the days of the Algonquin Roundtable. But opportunity is not what this story is about. This is a story of pain — of the precise kind of pain writers are heir to.

Read through the 43 worst moments, and if you come up with any you think I should add, let me know at www.jennienash.com.

Cheers! Jennie Nash

SECTION ONE

Agonies Before You Even Start

1.

YOU DEEM YOURSELF UNWORTHY

You have a burning desire to write a book – an idea that haunts you like a ghost in the attic — but you don't think you have the talent or the skill or the expertise to write it. "Who am I to write a book?" you ask. "I'm just a butcher, a baker, a candlestick maker." You cast around for someone to give you permission to write — a teacher, a friend who writes, a famous writer you met that one time at a signing, your mom — but no one ever gives you permission, because it's not their job. It's your job and you're not doing it. Your thoughts of unworthiness grow even deeper and stronger, until you believe it with your whole heart: you are not someone who can write a book. What were you even thinking? You take up tennis, knitting, become a voracious reader of other people's books — but the burning desire to write doesn't go away. It smolders there, often for a lifetime, turning into a jagged, hard-edged regret. "I always wanted to write a book," you say, and people smile their close-lipped smiles and quickly look away.

THE WAY FORWARD:

Stop looking outside for answers. Give yourself permission to create. You're the only one who can grant it, and the only one who can take it away.

If there are certain aspects about writing that you need to learn — certain skills you need to develop, certain elements you need to master — start practicing. They say it takes 10,000 hours to gain mastery in any given area, and they're not just talking about speaking French or performing brain surgery. They're talking about writing something strangers will want to read. You may have mastered some of these skills over the years through your day job, or by journaling, or by writing on the sly. For everything else, the clock starts now.

"There is no greater agony than bearing an untold story inside you."
— Maya Angelou

2.

YOU BELIEVE IN THE CABIN IN THE WOODS

You have a great idea for a book and you know it's going to be fantastic when you can find the time to write it, but that time never comes. Life, after all, is so full of emergencies. The dog gets sick, the stock market crashes, your best friend moves away, and just when it seems like things will settle down enough for you to start writing, your boyfriend gets sick, you crash the car into a fire hydrant, your dentist retires. You solve the new crop of problems, then head to Staples to buy a new notebook, some awesome gel pens, and some file folders to keep all the notes for your book straight — but on the way home your boss calls to say that you lost your biggest account, your mom calls to say that your grandma is ill and when you get home, you see that the big branch on the sycamore tree in the front yard has fallen on the neighbor's fence.

You start to dream about a quiet cabin in the woods where no one will disturb you while you set your story down on paper. You start looking at those neat grant programs that give writers their own cabins and a fat stipend, and lunch in a basket on the doorstep every day. That's what you need! You will apply for that program! You apply, but you don't get accepted. So you start looking for a time when you can go to one of those retreats in Italy or Mexico where you hang out with other writers, hammer out your book, and in the afternoons eat figs or mangos from the trees that hang over the pool. But you need $6,000 and a month off from work, and that never happens. It goes on like this for months on end, which turn into years on end, until your great idea dissolves into something as difficult to pin down as a dream.

THE WAY FORWARD:

For most of us, writing doesn't happen in a quiet cabin in the woods. There is no cabin, there are no woods. There is just the noise and the chaos and the pressure of life. If you are waiting for the mythical cabin, see the waiting for what it is — a form of procrastination. Then stop doing it. Acknowledge that life is busy and unpredictable and then find a way to make your writing a part of that busy, unpredictable life. Start by telling everyone you live with what you are doing so that they take it seriously, too — which is to say that they will give you space and time and support. Now write. No matter what else happens, just write.

"The hardest part of artmaking is living your life in such a way that your work gets done, over and over – and that means, among other things, finding a host of practices that are just plain useful. A piece of art is the surface expression of a life lived within productive patterns."

— *David Bayles,* Art & Fear: Observtions on the Perils (and Rewards) of Artmaking

3.

YOU BECOME PARALYZED BY THE FEAR OF FAILURE

You have a great idea for a book and you make the time to start in on it — and then you start thinking about what it would be like to fail. There are a thousand ways to fail!

You imagine spending hours every day sitting at your desk, writing, writing, writing — and never writing anything decent enough to show to anyone.

You imagine telling all your friends you're writing a book — and then having to tell them that, no, you're not; you couldn't hack it.

You imagine sending your work out to agents or editors and getting back an impersonal, thoughtless rejection. "We're sorry, but your work doesn't fit into our publishing plans at this time…."

You imagine giving up work, pay and productivity to get this book done — and never earning a dime for your efforts.

You imagine that you publish the book — and no one cares. It doesn't make a single ripple in the pond of the world. You end up with boxes of the book in your garage, where they yellow and mold along with your old tax returns.

You imagine that you publish the book — and it's raked over the coals on the cover of *The New York Times Book Review* and no one ever speaks of it again, although the fact of it sits there like an elephant in every room you enter.

You imagine your mother reading your book — and saying, "It was very interesting, Dear."

These images of failure become so vivid that you can't see beyond them. You become unable to write. You become unable to move forward. You quit.

THE WAY FORWARD:

Everyone is scared of failure. We live our whole lives trying to avoid failure, but to what end? None whatsoever. Stop thinking of fear as the enemy. Stop waiting for the fear to go away. Fear is an essential part of the process. If you're not scared, you're not likely to produce anything worthwhile.

"Are you paralyzed with fear? That's a good sign. Fear is good. Like self-doubt, fear is an indicator. Fear tells us what we have to do. Remember one rule of thumb: the more scared we are of a work or calling, the more sure we can be that we have to do it."

— *Steven Pressfield,* The War of Art

4.

YOU BECOME PARALYZED BY THE FEAR OF SUCCESS

You have a great idea, you start in on it — and then you start thinking about what it would be like to succeed. There are a thousand pitfalls inherent in success!

You're invited for an exclusive Oprah interview, but the last time you spoke in public your voice cracked so much and your hands shook so badly that they had to escort you away from the microphone. You spend weeks in utter agony, thousands of dollars on a TV-appropriate outfit, and thousands more dollars on media training. Once you get on air, your voice cracks and your hands shake and all Oprah wants to talk about are the scenes you prayed no one would really notice.

Your publisher is so excited about your Oprah appearance that they print an extra 100,000 copies of your book. Oprah forgets to mention the title, however, and she doesn't hold up the cover. 98,250 copies remain in the warehouse, and the book start to sell on Amazon.com for $0.1. The guy charging $3.99 for shipping is making a bigger margin than you are.

You get reviewed on the cover of *The New York Times Book Review* — and that creepy guy who lived across from you junior year gets in touch to say that he loves the portrait you painted of your abiding love and he is filing for divorce from his wife so he can come be by your side for eternity.

You make the bestseller list — and your friends start hitting you up for seed money for their new tech start-ups and African-based charities.

Your publisher is so excited about the bestseller list that they offer you $250,000 dollars for whatever book you write next. You take the money, but you don't have another idea. You are certain that you will never have another idea. You spend all the money on therapy, obessively work through *The Artist's Way*, dog-ear every page of *Art & Fear* and *The War of Art*, and still can't manage to produce even one page of prose. The publisher asks for the money back — which you no longer have, because you spent it on a new washing machine, a new car, a dive trip to Tahiti and a renovation of your home office.

Your mother calls to tell you that her book club is reading your book — and then she calls to say that she was mortified about that thing you wrote on page 45 and wonders how on earth could you trade the family's innermost secrets for money. She informs you that she is never speaking to you again.

The guy who sat next to you in a writing workshop fifteen years ago (the one who wore Ray-Ban aviators, never took off his puffy jacket, never shared any of his own work, and never spoke a single word to anyone) emails to say that your book idea was really his book idea — and you'll be hearing from his lawyer.

These images of success are so disturbing that you decide it's not worth it to move forward. Forget writing a book! You will take up kite surfing instead.

THE WAY FORWARD:

The class of problem you will have because of the wild success of your book is a much better class of problem than you will have toiling away in obscurity. Think of it as trading up. And stop using the perceived pitfalls of success as an excuse for not doing the work. Write your book, and if success comes, embrace it for all you're worth.

"Our deepest fear is not that we are inadequate. Our deepest fear is that we are powerful beyond measure. It is our light, not our darkness that most frightens us. We ask ourselves, 'Who am I to be brilliant, gorgeous, talented, fabulous?' Actually, who are you not to be."
—Marianne Williamson, Return to Love: Reflections on the Principles of "A Course in Miracles."

5.

YOU CAN'T COMMIT TO AN IDEA

You have so many brilliant ideas that it's hard to know where to start. There's the novel about the twin sisters and the novel about the corrupt lawyer, and then there's the memoir about how you lost all that weight and the memoir about med school, and then there's the business book about how to market to small businesses, which would be so good for your career. You have a chapter and an outline of each book — well, kind of an outline. You have a good solid sense of what the book is going to be about once you write the outline — and a good solid sense seems like it's enough. But it's not. When you sit down to write, you can never really get a grip on what you're doing, so you write a few pages, edit a few passages and then switch from project to project, zipping from one file to the other, amazed at the profusion of great ideas. But you don't move any one idea forward. You can't because committing to any one idea means that you'd have to leave the other excellent ideas behind. So you don't commit. You just keep adding projects to the hopper, paralyzed by your own brilliance.

THE WAY FORWARD:

People often ask writers and other creative people where they get their ideas. There's a sense that there's something mystical about getting an idea, or magic, or at least not exactly straightforward. Neil Gaiman has a wonderful quote about how he started answering the "where do you get your ideas?" question with the truth: "I make them up," he said, "Out of my head." But guess what? People didn't like this answer. They wanted something jazzier.

Willie Nelson once said, "The air is full of tunes; I just reach up and pick one." People new to writing, or to the creative life, may recognize the insistent idea, the shiny idea, the idea that's ripe for choosing, but they may not be comfortable committing to it. How do you know it's the right idea? What happens if it's the wrong idea? And what about the other ideas you are ignoring in favor of this one? The truth is that you will get no assurance. There will be no guarantee. David Hockney has the perfect answer for these dilemmas. He is talking about painting, but it applies just as well to writing: "Sometimes," he said, "I just begin."

"The acorn becomes an oak by means of automatic growth; no commitment is necessary. The kitten similarly becomes a cat on the basis of instinct. Nature and being are identical in creatures like them. But a man or woman becomes fully human only by his or her choices and his or her commitment to them. People attain worth and dignity by the multitude of decisions they make from day by day. These decisions require courage."

— Rollo May

6.

YOU TALK MORE THAN YOU WRITE

You are so into this whole writing thing that you talk about it everywhere to anyone, at all times and in all places. "I'm writing a book," you say to your colleagues and the postman and the guy who is resoling your shoes. When they ask what it's about, you have detailed answers. When they ask how it's going, you nod and say, "It's going well. It's hard work." When they tell you that it's a cool thing you're doing and that they always wanted to write a book, you say, "You should! It's fun!"

You sign up for a writing workshop at your local university, where you share a few pages and mostly talk about the writing process with your new writing friends. It's so much fun to be in a community of writers that you sign up for another course, share the same few pages, and meet some new writing friends. You also sign up for a blog where you get to talk about writing. And you start tweeting about writing, which is fun because it takes so little time.

At the holidays, your relatives ask what's new and you talk about your book. People give you writing-related gifts, like leather-bound journals, bookstore gift certificates, and special Post-It notes for your reading life. You love these gifts with all your heart because they validate that you are a writer.

But you're not really writing. You only have a few pages written. Some of those pages connect to other pages you've written, but not really. You start to feel like a fraud. An imposter. You realize that if you don't produce a book soon, people are going to find out your dirty little secret: that you don't really write. You only talk about it.

This will be so embarrassing. So you take a class in how to build a website and hire a graphic designer to make you a book cover. You make a website for your book, and this buys you a year or so of time, but at the end of the year, you have a website, not a book. Then this cool new yoga studio opens near you. They have this cool new class. It's all about getting centered. Anyone can get centered. It only takes an hour a few times a week. You finally stop talking about writing, and start talking about yoga instead.

THE WAY FORWARD:

Stop talking. Start writing. Just do it.

"If my doctor told me I had only six minutes to live, I wouldn't brood. I'd type a little faster."
— Isaac Asimov

SECTION TWO

The Agonies of Sitting Down and Actually Doing the Work

7.

IT'S LONELY AS HELL

You sit alone at your desk. Maybe it's 4:00 in the morning before anyone else gets up. Maybe it's 5:30 at the coffee shop down the street before you have to be at work. Maybe it's over your lunch hour or maybe it's at 10:00 at night after the kids have gone to bed. If you're lucky, and you've made some money at it and someone's paying you to write the next thing, maybe it's for 8 hours a day every day, or for 4 hours before you have to tweet your fans and answer the bloggers' interview questions and arrange to travel to Sun Valley for the writer's conference where you're going to speak. No matter what, it always ends up that you sit alone at your desk.

You fight to stay off the Internet — well, not off, because you need the Internet to research things and check things and stay connected to other people and see what other writers are up to. You fight to keep your time on the Internet in check.

You fight to stay away from the refrigerator, but the refrigerator beckons. There's the last slice of apple pie in there and some mushrooms in the bottom drawer that will go bad if you don't do something with them soon.

You fight to ignore the dishes and the laundry and bills piling up on the dining room table.

You fight to find your story.

And there's no one to talk to. No one who shares your excitement and your struggle. No one who knows that, although you spent four hours on one sentence, it was a good four hours. No one who knows that, although you wrote ten pages that day, it was a shitty day. You can tell people who ask how your day was that the writing went well or that it went badly, but unless they're other writers, they won't get it.

But even other writers won't really get it. They're working on their own stories, fighting their own urges, mired in their own doubts. They'll be nice to you and listen to you and nod and say vaguely pleasant things, and that will help for a while. But at the start of the day, every day, you have to face the fact that you have chosen to do work that is, by definition, lonely as hell.

THE WAY FORWARD:

Most would-be writers have a fundamental misunderstanding of what the job actually entails. Mostly, you sit alone in a room. Every so often, you may see a famous, bestselling writer under the bright lights, making witty comments and wearing great shoes, but when the show is over, that writer is going back to her quiet room and she's sitting there, alone, for several more years until her next book is done. It's exceedingly lonely work — and most people simply aren't comfortable being alone with themselves and their thoughts for that long. They fail simply because they like the idea of being a writer, but not the reality.

So, focus on the reality. Identify the steps needed to get the work done, and on the everyday satisfactions of doing it. Then go out and connect with other artists who speak your language and support your efforts. Maybe you do this by reading their books or looking at their art or listening to their music. Or maybe you do it by joining a group, finding a mentor. Loneliness goes with the territory, but it doesn't have to be the lord of the manor.

"What we do might be done in solitude and with great desperation, but it tends to produce exactly the opposite. It tends to produce community and in many people hope and joy."

— Junot Díaz

8.

THERE IS NO CORRECT ANSWER

You have no idea if what you're writing is any good. You have no idea if it even makes any sense. You start to think about math, and how in math there is always just one correct answer. You remember being a student sitting through lectures on long division and polynomial equations, and you consider that maybe those were the good old days. You daydream about jobs where there is a task that must be done – just one, tangible, quantifiable task — and someone telling you to do it. You start seeing those jobs everywhere, particularly at Trader Joe's, where the cashiers and the baggers and the guys who cut open the boxes in the back room all seem inordinately happy to be wearing their Hawaiian shirts and doing their jobs. Writing begins to seem like being trapped in a padded room. You quit before you go mad.

THE WAY FORWARD:

Trust your instincts. And remember that interesting experience or an interesting life does not automatically make for an interesting book. Stories need to be shaped, they need to make sense, they need to have a point — and writers, therefore, need to stand back and look at their ideas with a ruthless eye. You need to ask, "What's my story really about? And why would anyone care? And what's the best way to tell it?" And you need to come up with answers. Tom Clancy says, "The difference between fiction and reality is that fiction has to make sense."

The exact same thing can be said about memoir or narrative non-fiction, as well. A good idea is never enough, and there is no correct answer.

"All our progress is an unfolding, like a vegetable bud. You have first an instinct, then an opinion, then a knowledge as the plant has root, bud, and fruit. Trust the instinct to the end, though you can render no reason."
—Ralph Waldo Emerson

9.

THE WORLD DOESN'T REALLY NEED WHAT YOU'RE MAKING

Oh sure, there are all those awesome philosophies about art being the foundation of a good society, and art being more important than bread. It's easy to embrace those ideas when things are going well, but when they're not, it's just as easy to believe that they're phooey. You tune into the Presidential Election — to the conventions and the debates. You hear how it is. The politicians talk about real Americans — teachers and the guys who work the line at the auto plants and the Seal team who went in and stormed Osama bin Laden's hideout. The politicians talk about entrepreneurs and innovators, small business people who create jobs. They don't talk about novelists or the people who sit at their computers and write moving memoirs. Because while it's all well and good to believe in the sustaining power of books, the sustaining power of schools and bridges will trump books every time.

THE WAY FORWARD:

Remember the stories that have brought you solace, inspiration, entertainment, knowledge and a sense of community, and remember that their creators felt the same doubt you did.
Imagine the loss if they had stopped because no one asking for their story? Use this memory of books you love to fuel your work.

"Works of art provide us with individual satisfaction: a sense of release, pleasure and reflection. And they act as a focal point around which we can share and dispute meanings. Art helps us to understand what we have in common and where we differ, what we like and what offends us, what excites us and what leaves us cold. We come together around art without having to agree about it... Without art we would find it increasingly difficult to convey our innermost feeling. Imagine a world without color, rhyme or melody: it's bleak beyond belief."

— Peter Hewitt

10.

YOUR KIDS (OR YOUR DOG) SCARE AWAY THE MUSE

Your kids (or your dog) are loud, demanding, ever-present, and needy. Don't they realize that the muse is a fragile thing? That you have to tiptoe around her, whisper in her presence and barely breathe lest she disappear? Don't they understand that you are courting the muse and that the muse has a choice whether or not she sticks around? No they do not. Your kids come into your writing space with peanut butter on their fingers, pulling each other's hair, screaming, yelling, whining, crying and whimpering — and voila! The muse is gone. You knew it would happen like that. It always does. You hate the muse and in that moment, you hate your kids, too.

THE WAY FORWARD:

Stop looking for other people, things, or spirits to blame. The muse is you, and you are awesome. Come up with a solution to get your work done: feed the older ones copious amounts of ice cream and plant them in front of the TV. Try to ignore the incredibly irritating music, the laugh track, and the character who speaks in a voice so grating it could sink ships. Put the little ones in a warm bathtub with a bunch of toys and sit just outside the bathroom door on the floor in the hallway where you will hear them if they start to drown.

Now you get five minutes peace to finish your scene or at least your sentence.

"Creativity and inspiration don't come from some place outside of you, and they aren't really `out-of-the-blue.' They're the result of years of hard work, of having the grit and determination to stick to your craft, of hard-won lessons about the way story works."

— *Lisa Cron,* Wired for Story

11.

YOU HATE EVERYTHING YOU WRITE

You read all the books about writing habits and you adopt a few habits that seem particularly smart. One of them is to write 1,000 words a day, and to start each day reviewing the 1,000 words from the day before. So you write 1,000 words on the first day. On the second day, you read those words and decide they suck — they are so very far from the vision you had in your head, and so very far from the kind of writing you love to read — and so you delete them in one quick "Select All/Delete" motion, and write 1,000 new words. On the third day you read the new words and decide they suck, too. You can't believe how badly they suck and so you delete them. On day four, you write another 1,000, but they, too, are no good. By the end of the week you have written 7,000 words, but none of them were worth keeping and so you have precisely nothing. The conclusion can only be one thing: you will never be a writer.

THE WAY FORWARD:

Be gentle with yourself, and find a writing practice that doesn't make you crazy. Writing 1,000 words a day may work for some people, but if it doesn't work for you, it's a waste of time and energy. Once you have the habit of writing, don't expect the doubt about your work to magically disappear. It doesn't ever disappear. I have friends who are mega-selling authors, and friends who are mega-award-winning authors and they all say that the doubt doesn't actually get any better the more you succeed. It gets worse; the only difference is that the seasoned pro expects the doubts and doesn't let it crush them. The seasoned pro just keeps putting words on the page, slowly building a world, and once they have a critical mass, they assess the words and look for ways to improve them. As Susan Bell says in The Artful Edit, "We write into a void, but we edit in a universe."

"If you find yourself asking yourself (and your friends), "Am I really a writer? Am I really an artist?" chances are you are. The counterfeit innovator is wildly self confident. The real one is scared to death."
— Steven Pressfield, The War of Art

12.

YOU LOSE AN ENTIRE MANUSCRIPT BECAUSE YOU SPILL MONKEY-PICKED OOLONG TEA ON YOUR KEYBOARD

There is one brief moment of clarity, where you know exactly what has happened and exactly what has been lost, and then there is utter despair. The kind of despair that leads directly to a bottle of vodka. Or divorce. Because while your spouse can make the earth shake in bed and make a mean lasagna and do the taxes and dance the mamba, he cannot make your manuscript reappear and you hate him for it. You also hate the genius that sold you the computer, and you hate Steve Jobs, even though he's dead. You especially hate your neighbor who's been telling you about getting a backup hard drive, signing up for Carbonite, sending everything to the cloud and other nonsense that might — just might — have saved you in your time of need. Why didn't that guy make you *do* those things? What kind of a friend just stands by while you walk straight into the darkness? You pick up something breakable and throw it. It feels good, so you do it again. Soon your house is trashed, just like your marriage and your hopes and dreams for a better life. You will never write again. Never.

THE WAY FORWARD:

Be a grown up about your work. Get a back up hard drive, have a double-safe system that backs up to the web, and learn how to use them.

"The real problem is not whether machines think but whether men do.

— B. F. Skinner

13.

YOUR FRIENDS WON'T LEAVE YOU ALONE

They know you're at home writing — and so you're a sitting duck. You're asked to have lunch, do afternoon carpool, sit on the committee for a fundraising event, have lunch, play tennis, sign up, have lunch. You're so busy fielding requests that you can't get any work done, and since you can't get any work done, you figure you might as well go out to lunch. You go to lunch and your friends ask how the book is coming. "Okay," you say, "a little slower than I'd like." Your friends smile. "You know what you should do when it's done?" they say, "You should get Oprah to pick it for her book club." You laugh and say, "I'll do that." The next time your friends ask you out to lunch, you gather your resolve and say that you're busy. It's not that you don't like them; it's just that, if you're going to get into Oprah's book club, you really need to get some work done. But then another friend calls and asks if you want to play tennis, and the vicious cycle continues.

THE WAY FORWARD:

Turn off the Internet connection, turn off the phone, and just say no. In order to write, you have to be willing to give something up. Think about it: if you're going to take on a new habit of writing every day, or writing every other day, or writing 10 pages a week, you're going to have to give up something else that used to fill that time, and you're going to have to say no. A lot.

"Be ruthless about protecting writing days, i.e., do not cave in to endless requests to have "essential" and "long overdue" meetings on those days. The funny thing is that, although writing has been my actual job for several years now, I still seem to have to fight for time in which to do it. Some people do not seem to grasp that I still have to sit down in peace and write the books, apparently believing that they pop up like mushrooms without my connivance. I must therefore guard the time allotted to writing as a Hungarian Horntail guards its firstborn egg."

— J.K. Rowling

14.

ANOTHER WRITER WRITES YOUR BOOK BEFORE YOU FINISH WRITING YOUR BOOK

You're toiling away at your novel about Abraham Lincoln, thinking you're really on a roll now, when you open the *Wall Street Journal* and there on the "Off Duty" page is a round-up of great books about Abraham Lincoln, collected by the author of a forthcoming novel about Abraham Lincoln. You Google the author and learn that he is one of the world's foremost experts on Abraham Lincoln, and holds a special endowed chair on Abraham Lincoln at the Woodrow Wilson School at Princeton. He just happens to write fiction in his spare time on Tuesdays, and that effort has resulted in this great new novel. You click around and notice that the expert's book has recently been reviewed by Terry Gross on Fresh Air and optioned for a movie by Steven Spielberg. Then you shut your computer down, go eat a big slice of chocolate cake, get in bed and pull the covers over your head. When your loved ones ask you what's wrong you yell, "Why the fuck do you think anything's wrong?"

The next time you log onto your computer, you take the draft of your novel about Lincoln and slip it into the archives. You will try to forget about it, but you will now see the other person's Lincoln book everywhere. It will be stacked a mile high at Costco, displayed in the window of your local independent bookstore, lovingly set on the coffee table of your best friend's ski lodge. The blurbs on the cover will taunt you and that stupid portrait of Lincoln peering out at you as if he knows what you have failed to do. When your book club decides to read the Lincoln book, you bow out. When people start talking about it at cocktail parties, you grit your teeth. You have to go to the dentist and get one of those mouth guards to protect your teeth from sure destruction. And of course the dentist will have the Lincoln book on the side table for his patient's reading pleasure.

THE WAY FORWARD:

Take a deep breath and keep writing.

And note that there have been 15,000 books written about Abraham Lincoln. There is room for one more. There is always room for one more.

"So this is always the key: you have to write the book you love, the book that's alive in your heart. That's the one you have to write."
— Lurleen McDaniel

15.

YOU DEVELOP NECK PAIN, SUFFER FROM CARPEL TUNNEL, AND GAIN FIFTEEN POUNDS OF FAT

Dr. Oz says that humans weren't made to sit as long as we sit. You shouldn't sit at a desk or work a computer for more than a few minutes at a time. You should get up and do jumping jacks, and sit-ups, and deep breathing. But you don't, because you have this book to finish. You sit so long that your butt goes numb, your fingers tingle, and your eyesight starts to get weird. You go to the eye doctor who amps up your prescription and gives you a special deal on the anti-reflective coating that will make everything better — only $1,400 for each lens. You go to your regular doctor to ask about the tingling, and she tells you that surgery is the only solution and that you should stop working so many hours at the computer, and then when you're about to leave, she looks at the chart and says that you're fifteen pounds heavier than you were last year. "How's your exercise program going?" she asks. You lie and say that it's going fine, when, in fact, your only exercise is standing up and going to the refrigerator. "Keep it up," she says, and you go home, have a bowl of Ben and Jerry's Cherry Garcia, pop a few Advil, and keep writing.

THE WAY FORWARD:

Make exercise part of writing your routine. There is abundant evidence — both scientific and anecdotal — that physical fitness and mental fitness go hand in hand. So sit your butt in the chair and write. Then get up and get moving. It's as simple — and profound — as that.

"For me, writing is a discipline, much like playing a musical instrument. It requires constant practice and honing of skills…If I'm not at my desk by sunrise, I feel like I'm missing my most productive hours. In addition to starting early, I keep an antique hourglass on my desk and every hour break briefly to do push-ups, sit-ups and quick stretches. This helps keep the blood, and ideas, flowing."

— Dan Brown

SECTION THREE

The Agonies of Sharing Work in Progress

16.

YOU REFUSE TO LET YOUR WORK OUT OF YOUR SIGHT

You finished your book! You have read it so many times you feel like you could recite it out loud from memory. You have this niggling little voice inside you that says, "This is the best damn thing anyone has ever created. It's going to rock the world!" You naturally want to test your theory, and you start thinking of people you can send it to who will be straightforward and generous in their assessment of your work. You can't think of anyone who meets the qualifications. People can be so mean! And so ruthless! You don't think you can bear mean and ruthless, so you decide to keep revising. You go back to page one, and fiddle around with some commas and sentences, and then you go to page two. You do this in an endless cycle for years, until one day you stop, and your book just sits there, unseen by anyone's eyes but your own.

THE WAY FORWARD:

Remember that, unless your goal is simply self-expression, the point of writing is to be read. Send the book out and don't take the feedback personally. It may be your heart and soul on the page, but to everyone else, it's just words that may or may not have any meaning or resonance.

Listen to what they're saying, and decide whether or not to do anything about it. You are the god of your own story.

"I went for years not finishing anything. Because, of course, when you finish something you can be judged... I had poems which were re-written so many times I suspect it was just a way of avoiding sending them out."

— Erica Jong

17.

YOU ASK SOMEONE YOU LOVE TO READ YOUR BOOK WITH THE ERRONEOUS ASSUMPTION THAT THEY WILL LOVE IT AS MUCH AS THEY LOVE YOU

You give the book to your wife. She puts the manuscript on her bedside table, on top of *Fifty Shades of Gray*. Every night, for weeks, you watch as she grabs the steamy novel — and the sequel and the other sequel — instead of your manuscript. Finally, unable to stand it anymore, you remove the manuscript from her reading pile. She doesn't notice, and you decide that you hate her with all your heart.

THE WAY FORWARD:

Keep the people you love away from your writing. They love you — isn't that enough? You can't expect them to love your writing, too — and chances are that if they do love it, it's blind love, not a useful love that can help you craft a better story. People you love aren't automatically part of your fan base. Loving you and loving your work are two entirely different things.

Now start searching for someone who loves you as a writer. This is not permission to have an illicit Internet (or other) affair.

This is a directive to find a writing peer. A pal. A colleague. She's out there. Go find her.

"The opposite of love isn't hate; it's indifference."
— *Steven Pressfield,* The War of Art

18.

YOU ASK A WRITER FRIEND TO READ YOUR WORK WITH THE ERRONEOUS ASSUMPTION THAT THEY WILL HELP YOU MAKE IT BETTER

"It's pretty good for a rough draft," the writer says, "but what would really help is if you make Tiffany a boy, and make Julianne a samurai warrior because then you could have a bank heist in the end instead of, you know, that love scene." You smile and thank him for his feedback, even though you realize that the feedback had nothing to do with what you wrote and everything to do with the thriller your writer friend is writing.

THE WAY FORWARD:

You may have to look hard and wide, but find writer friends who know how to respond to the sentence, "For now, can you just tell me that it's okay?" (The correct answer is, "Yes. It's wonderful. Keep going." Unless, of course, it's not wonderful, in which case the correct answer is, "It's wonderful, but it could be better. I know you can do it.")

Also, hire an editor or book coach.

Paying a professional to pay rapt attention to your work-in-progress is the most direct path to getting someone to pay rapt attention to your work-in-progress.

"Writers in their natural state are about as civilized as feral cats."

— *Theresa Rebeck,* Seminar

19.

YOU ASK A FRIEND WHO IS AN ENGLISH TEACHER TO READ YOUR WORK WITH THE ERRONEOUS ASSUMPTION THAT THEY WILL HELP MAKE IT BETTER

"I really enjoyed it, except for your misuse of the semi colon," the English teacher says. You smile at this faint praise, and that opens the floodgates. "You know, there were also some spelling issues in Chapter 5," she says, "and in Chapter 10 I think you mishandled the timing of that holiday dinner. It was 18 days after Thanksgiving, not 17." You smile and thank her for her feedback, but inside there is a hard knot of resentment. Does she not understand the craft of writing? Does she think that punctuation is the be-all and end-all of written communication? She goes on. "I actually wrote up 14 pages of notes about errors you made. I'll email it to you." You feel completely and wholly misunderstood because now you are going to have to worry about 267 points of punctuation when what you really wanted to know right now was if the ending worked.

THE WAY FORWARD:

Smart writers ask for the exact kind of feedback they need from their readers. Do you want to know if the ending was satisfying? Ask for that. Do you want to know if the beginning is intriguing? Ask for that. If you want specific feedback on a time period, or a location, or the flow of information, or the overall arc, ask for that. Choose your readers depending on what they can, and are able and willing to provide. Ask if the reader can provide you with that, in the time frame that you need. If they can't, find another reader. Or hire an editor. And when it's time for a proofreader to catch every last grammatical error in your work, you have two choices: get a contract with a traditional publisher who employs such people, or hire one yourself.

"To those who care about punctuation, a sentence such as "Thank God its Friday" (without the apostrophe) rouses feelings not only of despair but of violence. The confusion of the possessive "its" (no apostrophe) with the contractive "it's" (with apostrophe) is an unequivocal signal of illiteracy and sets off a Pavlovian "kill" response in the average stickler."

— *Lynne Truss,* Eats, Shoots & Leaves: The Zero Tolerance Approach to Punctuation

SECTION FOUR

The Agonies of Revising

20.

YOU FIGURE OUT THE BOOK YOU'RE TRYING TO WRITE ONLY WHEN YOU GET TO "THE END"

You're so excited because after years of hard work, you finally have a finished draft of your book. You print it out, go to a lovely coffee shop where other writers are hard at work, and feeling as if you're about to rise above all of them because of your diligence, determination and general awesomeness, you begin to read your pages. You read all the way through from page 1 to "The End" and in the last fifteen pages, you have a revelation that is exactly like being hit by a bolt of lightning: your book is not about how the course of true love never did run smooth. It is, in fact, about how it is better to have loved and lost than never to have loved at all.

You sit back in your chair, jaw hanging open, and smack yourself on the forehead. You chuckle. "Wow," you say out loud. No one looks up from their laptops, because they think you're insane. You order a triple mocha latte with an extra shot of espresso, go back to page 1, and start thinking about how to bring out the theme of your book. You see right away that it's delicate work. It's a word here, a gesture there. It's body language and transitions. *This is cake*, you think, *I'll be done by 5:00.* But at 5:00, you're still on page 1. You realize that it is going to take months and months and months to recalibrate the whole book to the new world order, and you have no choice but to do it. You have the burden of knowledge; you know what you're actually trying to say and you can see in every sentence that you haven't yet said it.

THE WAY FORWARD:

Writing bubbles up from many layers of consciousness. There's the hyper-critical consciousness that babbles in our ear all the time telling us to give it up; the logical consciousness that helps us resolve a conflict on page 205 that we launched on page 10; and the creative consciousness that helps us decide how to describe the way the sunlight filtered through the trees. Running underneath all these layers is our unconscious, which, by definition, we're not even aware of. Our unconscious has probably been in the drivers' seat of our story from minute one, but we don't know it. We can't see it, can't hear it, can't access it. Once we figure out a way to do so (more on this in a moment), we can go back to our story and weave it together in a way that makes everything snap, crackle and pop with meaning.

Get used to it: this is the creative process.

"Books aren't written—they're rewritten. Including your own. It is one of the hardest things to accept, especially after the seventh rewrite hasn't quite done it."

— Michael Crichton

21.

YOU WOULD RATHER DIE THAN FACE THE TRUTH ABOUT YOUR WORK

You get some feedback that resonates with you —which is to say, it feels like a gong going off in your head. You knew from the start that you should have started your book with the scene in Istanbul, but you wrote 70 pages about everything that happened in Prague, instead, because you were scared to go straight to the heart of your story. So when five readers mention that the first 70 pages are slow and that things really pick up when you get to Istanbul, you know what must happen – but you don't dare do it. There must be a way to save all those months and months of work! You go back in and spend months trying to make the first 70 pages fit, trying to beef them up, amp them up, make them so whiz-bang that no one would dare suggest they need to go — but every time you read the pages, there is a place deep inside you that knows you are wrong. So you are at war with yourself, and your book is the battleground.

THE WAY FORWARD:

Get rid of what isn't working. Your job is to serve the story, not your ego.

"Put down everything that comes into your head and then you're a writer. But an author is one who can judge his own stuff's worth, without pity, and destroy most of it."
— Colette

22.

YOU REALIZE THAT YOUR BOOK HAS A FATAL FLAW

You are 47 pages into writing a new book, or perhaps it's 123 or 319. You print out the pages and give them to a trusted reader, who, instead of calling you to say how brilliant your work is, or how great this book is, or how awesome you are, leaves a message saying, "I read the pages. Call me when you get a chance." You know the news is bad. You're thinking that maybe you have to ax the first 70 pages, or recalibrate what the book is really about. *I can do this,* you think. *I got this.* After all, you love your book. You've put everything you have into making it. You're not going give up on it now just because the going gets tough. So you call your friend back and ask her to give it to you straight.

"I hate the main character," she says.

Okay, you're thinking. *This is fixable.*

"Hate how?" you ask.

Your friend launches into a diatribe about what narcissistic, self centered bitch your heroine is, and how she actually wanted to throw the book across the room, and how nothing makes sense with a main character who is so flawed.

"I could rewrite the first three chapters," you suggest.

Your friend laughs. "But she's a bitch in chapter 5 and 7 and 23, too."

You nod. "Maybe I could just tone her down a little?"

Your friend laughs. "But your whole premise is that she's a bitch. It's about being a bitch. It's just that no one wants to read about someone so bitchy."

You thank her for your time and give the manuscript to twelve other people to read. They all say the same thing: the woman is a bitch and no one wants to read about a woman who is such a bitch.

You determine all your readers are insane so you ignore them and send the book out to six agents, who you are longing to work with. Four of them don't reply. One sends back a form letter rejection. The sixth writes a note: "Your writing is good, but may want to re-think your premise. It's hard for readers to identify with a main character who is so narcissistic and self centered."

You quietly move the file off your desktop and tell yourself you'll revisit it in a few weeks – but you never do. You never open that file again.

THE WAY FORWARD:

Take a deep breath and fix it. Or throw the whole thing out and start something else. This is what writers do.

When you write a book, you spend day after day scanning and identifying the trees. When you're done, you have to step back and look at the forest."

— *Stephen King,* On Writing

SECTION FIVE

The Agonies of Submitting the Work to Agents

23.

YOU'RE TOO CHICKEN TO SUBMIT

You have been working on your book for 17 years. You have rewritten it so many times that every word is polished to a high shine. The thing virtually glows. You have sent it out for feedback, responded to the feedback, read it out loud word for word in front of the mirror. It is finished — and yet, you find a word to change here, a comma to change there. You wake up in the middle of the night and decide to change your main character's name. You're driving on the 405 towards Sunset and realize that your opening sentence stinks, so you craft a new one, and spend three weeks getting it just right. When people ask if you're still working on that book, you nod and knit your brow and say, "Yes, absolutely. It's getting there." But it's not getting there, because you won't let it go. You've tied an anchor on it and sunk that anchor in the muck. You have become this thing you always wanted to be — someone who finished a book — but you are unable to risk the humiliation, embarrassment, and failure of making it public, and so you don't. And when you are old and looking back on your life, you will think of that book — of the beautiful words, the artful sentences — and you will regret that you never gave it a chance.

THE WAY FORWARD:

Go onto agentquery.com and find an agent who is accepting unsolicited queries. Make sure it's an agent who represents the kinds of books you write. Write a query letter to an agent you admire. Send it off. Repeat. After about 6 rejections, see if there is any pattern to the feedback you are getting. See if there is anything that can be revised. Revise it, and then send out the book again. Repeat this 9 times.

"Talent is helpful in writing, but guts are absolutely essential."

— Jessamyn Wes

24.

YOU SUBMIT AND THEN HEAR NOTHING BUT THE SOUND OF SILENCE

You carefully select an agent, read every word on her website, and her blog, pour over interviews she's given at conferences, and craft a query that you believe accurately and enthusiastically represents you and your book. You hit 'send.' For the next three hours, you sit at your computer hitting the 'refresh' button, scouring your inbox for a response. None comes. You go back onto the agent's site and re-read her FAQs. It said right there that you may hear anywhere from within 30 seconds to never. The 30 seconds didn't happen, but surely the never won't be your fate. *Never*? You check the inbox again — and you repeat this pattern every day for a week. You start to get surly at dinnertime. You feel tempted to hurl your computer into the street. Your head begins to buzz.

You go out onto Google and search for things about the agent. You stumble upon a blog post in which the agent recounts the story of falling in love with a query and calling the writer within thirty seconds to offer representation, and how the agent was sure the book would be a bestseller, and now here they are, with a multi-million dollar deal that closed this very day.

You send your query out to the second agent on your list – and wait and wait and wait. *Never*? That seems to be your fate. So you stop sending out your book. Who, after all, needs this humiliation?

THE WAY FORWARD:

The minute you send your book out into the world, it is no longer a creative work of art; it is a product that will be bought and sold. You are an entrepreneur, and sometimes in business things take longer than you would like them to take. Steel yourself for what might possibly be a long wait and then write something else.

"This manuscript of yours that has just come back from another editor is a precious package. Don't consider it rejected. Consider that you've addressed it 'to the editor who can appreciate my work' and it has simply come back stamped 'not at this address.' Just keep looking for the right address."
— Barbara Kingsolver

25.

YOU ARE REJECTED AS HARD AS A LOVESICK TEENAGER HOPING FOR A DATE TO THE DANCE

The rejections pour in like a torrential flood, and they are curt and rude and mean, and it seems as if no one even read a page of the story that you ripped right out of your heart. You want to get on a plane and go to New York and march up to every one of these agents and pump your fist and say, "What do you know, you worthless punk?" But you don't, because you know what they do to people like that – which is throw restraining orders at them. So you delete all the rejections, and you delete the manuscript, and when anyone asks you how your book is going, you shrug and say, "I'm going to run a marathon, instead."

You have a good laugh with the person, until they say, "What about self publishing? My cousin's friend made a mint with her paranormal romance historical fiction series." Now you never want to see this person again. Because what they don't understand is that you just endured flat-out cold rejection, and that there is the teeny, tiniest possibility that all those agents were right and that your book sucks, and the last thing you want is to put it into the marketplace and have a bunch of clueless readers who are clamoring for historical paranormal romances decide that your book is worthless. So you walk away and you go on a run. And when your running pals praise your stride, you beam. *See, fuckers*, you think, *I'm all over this.*

THE WAY FORWARD:

Look up on the Internet all the awesome stories about great books that got rejected hundreds of times and then keep sending out your manuscript. Send it out 50 times, 100 times. If you still have nothing but 100 rejections, put it away for six months, and then sit down and look hard at what you have written. Do you still love it? Do you still think it's commercial viable. If so, consider whether there is anything you can change about your query, your opening chapters, your middle or your end to make it stronger, and if there is, change it. Then submit again. If the answer is no — you don't love it, you don't think it's commercially viable, then count up the hours you worked on that book, and consider them bankable hours towards the 10,000 you need to master your craft. Then start a new book.

"Rejection leads to a swiftly-experienced version of the five stages of grief: denial, anger, bargaining, depression, and acceptance. It's key to get to that last step as quickly as you can reckon. I actually have two additional steps in my personal process: "liquor" and "ice cream." Your mileage may vary."

— Chuck Wendig

26.

YOU LAND AN AGENT YOU LOVE, BUT HE WANTS TO SPEND "A LITTLE TIME" TWEAKING YOUR MANUSCRIPT

"A little time" turns out to be six months of back-breaking revision. The agent has a totally different vision of your book than you do – a darker vision — but you want to sell it, and so you bend. You do what she asks. There's a nagging little voice inside your head that keeps saying, *"This isn't the book I wanted to write, this doesn't feel good, I'm not so sure about this,"* but you press on writing the book your agent wants you to write, because you want it to sell, but with every passing moment, you feel like a sell-out. If you did everything this woman asked, it would take it to the end of that line, to a place where evil lives — the evil that comes from losing yourself.

You realize with horror that you can't do it. You can't go there. You tell the agent you must decline the offer. She yells and screams and says that you will never have lunch in this town again. You know that to be true, but you have no choice. You put everything having to do with the book into a file on your computer, send it to the archives and start thinking about a job teaching kids how to surf. It's pure, it's good. Who doesn't like to be in the sunshine learning a new skill? You start missing your deadlines. Your agent's voice becomes clipped and cold. You stop returning her emails. When it's time to upgrade your computer to a new whiz-bang platform, you don't do it. You buy a custom-shaped surfboard instead.

THE WAY FORWARD:

Never compromise your vision for the book. Don't work with people who don't share your vision. You may indeed have to spend six months revising with your agent, but only do it if it feels right. Remember: you are the god of your own story.

"Vision without action is a daydream. Action without vision is a nightmare."
— Japanese proverb

SECTION SIX

The Agonies of Submitting the Work to Publishers

27.

YOU GET AN OFFER FOR LESS MONEY THAN YOU TYPICALLY SPEND ON ONE MONTH OF GROCERIES

You worked on your book for four years. You got up early before work, stayed up late at the end of the day. You spent hundreds of dollars on ink and paper, an ergonomic chair and a footrest. You read the writing blogs, took a writing class, and sacrificed your family vacation to take a workshop with a novelist you love. You got an agent, and spent hundreds of dollars on good champagne and chocolate mousse cake for all your friends. The agent sends your book out to 47 editors. 46 reject it, but one comes back with an offer of $2,000.00. You could turn it down and self publish, but it's not just any publisher. It's the awesome publisher of Hemingway, Fitzgerald, Faulkner, JK Rowling, Stephen King and Stephanie Meyer. For the rest of your life you will be able to say, "My book was published by Awesome Publisher," and you will get to see people nod their heads at the awesomeness of it. That head-nodding is worth a lot, and so you say yes. By the time your agent takes her cut and you pay taxes, you have enough money to buy groceries for your family for a month. At the end of the month, Awesome Publisher starts saying they'd like to see book #2 ASAP. So you set your alarm, and get up before work, and do it all again.

THE WAY FORWARD:

Be thankful and carry on. Self publish. Or get a job bagging groceries at Trader Joe's instead.

"The profession of book-writing makes horse racing seem like a solid, stable business."
— John Steinbeck

28.

YOU GET AN OFFER FROM AN EDITOR WHO ADORES YOUR BOOK, AND WHO PROMPTLY QUITS

She thought you were the next big thing. She thought you were a genius. But she's going to have a baby, or she got a better offer from a competing publisher, or she decided to head off to Maine to write the novel she always wanted to write. No matter what the reason, you are now a publishing orphan. The person who loved your book and championed it and brought it to the publishing house is gone. No one else on staff really knows who you are. They assign your book to another editor, who writes you a nice note and in it asking what your book is about.

THE WAY FORWARD:

Take a deep breath, smile, and tell the nice editor what your book is about.

"Writing a book is a very lonely business. You are totally cut off from the rest of the world, submerged in your obsessions and memories."
— Mario Vargas Llosa

29.

YOU ALMOST WIN THE LITERARY LOTTERY — AND THEN YOU DON'T WIN ANYTHING AT ALL

Random House calls your agent. They love your book. Simon and Schuster calls. They love your book, too. Little Brown, Algonquin, Knopf and Hachette all call. They all love the book. Your agent sets an auction date, and tells you that no news is good news. You find it hard to sleep. You find it hard to breathe. You find it hard not to think of all the ways you will spend the vast amounts of money that will soon be coming your way. You can pay off your mortgage! Fund your children's college educations! Maybe finally take a real vacation.

On the day of the auction, you leap out of bed and have four cups of coffee. You sit and stare at the phone, willing it to ring. You imagine what you will do when you get the news — who you will call first, what you will say. You wonder if you will cry. The phone rings and it's a company offering specials on heating duct cleaning. You say no thank you and hang up. The phone rings a second later and it's a company wanted you to take five minutes to do a survey on your grocery shopping habits. You don't even say no thank you this time before you hang up. Finally, at 11:30, your agent calls. You hold your breath while she speaks. She's so very sorry, she says. They all pulled out in the end. They just couldn't get the support they needed.

You give some sort of reply that indicates that you will be fine, but you are not fine. You are so not fine. You will not be fine for a long time to come.

THE WAY FORWARD:

Howl at the moon, throw a plate against the wall, pour yourself a shot or two of whiskey and then start looking hard for the silver lining.

"Ones best success comes after their greatest disappointments."
— Harriet Ward Beecher

SECTION SEVEN

The Agonies of Working Well With Others

30.

YOUR BOOK COVER MAKES YOU CRY

Your editor says that the art department has been working obsessively on a cover for your book and they hope to have something soon. Everyone in the publishing house is so excited about the cover and they just know you're going to love it. The anticipation is killing you, and you basically stop sleeping as you lie in wait for the FedEx guy. Then one day, the FedEx truck pulls up in front of your house and the FedEx guy trots up to the door and hands you an envelope. You stand in your doorway, tearing it open — and there is the most hideous, incorrect, ugly, just plain wrong interpretation of your book that you could have ever imagined. You call your agent and beg her to go in and argue on your behalf, but odds are good it won't do any good. The art department loves the cover. The sales team loves the cover. The publisher loves the cover. You accept your fate because you have no other choice – but every time you see the cover on a website you cringe. Every time you see the book on the bookshelf of a bookstore you cringe. When readers say, "I almost didn't pick up your book because of the cover," you smile a sick little smile and say, "I know what you're saying." But still that cover lives. It will be a part of your life for eternity.

THE WAY FORWARD:

Self publish, so then you have no one to blame but yourself.

"There is no accounting for tastes."
— Proverb

31.

YOUR PUBLISHER'S PUBLICIST, WHO CAN'T BE OLDER THAN TWELVE, DOES NOTHING TO HELP YOUR CAUSE

You turn in an Author Questionnaire 45 pages long. It details all the contacts you have at journals, magazines and websites; gives a detailed list of pithy commentary you can make on radio and TV; offers ten pages of guest post possibilities at major blogs; provide the names of forty seven influential people who are willing to read the galleys; and outlines eighteen conferences at which your keynote address would be a fresh, exciting and effective addition. You explain that you have six months and $20,000 set aside to publicize your book. You will speak! You will sign! You will travel! Your publicist tells you that you are amazing. She thanks you for all your hard work. She says she is working on a press release. You never hear from her again.

THE WAY FORWARD:

Roll up your sleeves and get to work making your own connections, with readers, one at a time. It's your book, and no one else will love it as much as you do. You are, therefore, the best advocate for it.

You might start by hiring an outside publicist who you think is awesome, and whose track record in getting attention for books is awesome, too.

Some are born great, some achieve greatness, and some hire public relations officers."

— Daniel J. Boorstin

SECTION EIGHT

The Agonies of Self Publishing

32.

THERE ARE 1,237 DECISIONS TO MAKE AND NO ONE TO HELP YOU MAKE THEM

Self publishing is so much fun! You get total control! You can design your own cover, insert a cool little graphic at the start of each chapter, give the book away for free for three days, price it at $.99 one day and $24.99 the next, hold contests, run twitter campaigns, undertake a blog tour, do a book signing every day for a month and throw a bad-ass book launch party with book-themed food and cases of champagne. You don't have to get anyone's permission to do anything! It's so awesome!

And then it becomes exhausting. Does your book description sound stupid? Do readers hate your cover? Is $.99 too low? Is $24.99 too high? Do contests work? Is your money better spent on ads or a party? Someone asks you what you want for dinner, and you bite their head off. Someone asks you if you'd rather play golf or tennis, and you hang up on them. Someone asks you what you're writing next and you laugh and say, "*Writing next?* Who has time to write??"

THE WAY FORWARD:

Get good at making decisions, hire people to help, or write a book traditional publishers believe will sell.
And remember what it was like when writers had no other options.

"Opportunity is missed by most people because it is dressed in overalls and looks like work."
— Thomas Edison

33.

YOU ARE NO DIFFERENT THAN CRAZY CAT LADY AT THE END OF THE BLOCK

When you can say, "My third novel is being published by Penguin," you are not just a wanna-be hopeful novelist. You are legit! You are chosen! Pitching book reviewers is a breeze. Attending high school reunions is a delight. When you run into more famous writers, you meet as colleagues, exchanging e-mails, making dates for lunch. But when you self publish, you are no different than the crazy cat lady down the block who has been working on her memoir for 17 years or the guy at the street fair hawking Xeroxed pamphlets of his poetry about fruit. People smile indulgently when you tell them what you're doing. Book reviewers politely decline. Your doubts about writing, which you've spent a lifetime overcoming, blossom like a drug-resistant virus.

THE WAY FORWARD:

Find a way to rise above the cat lady — like, say, a loyal following of devoted readers. Or write a book the traditional publishers believe will sell. Whatever you do, don't stop writing.

"You fail only if you stop writing."
—Ray Bradbury

34.

YOU SPEND MORE MONEY THAN YOU MAKE

You buy a super cool advertising package that's going to put your book in front of 5 million eager readers. It costs $750. You sell 40 e-books at $2.99 each.

You participate in a super cool book fair that's going to put you in front of 5 million eager book readers. It costs you $250, plus you have to buy a new pair of jeans and a cool shirt to wear so you don't go in your pajamas, and that puts you out another $350. You sell 10 paperback books for $12.95.

You sign up for a super cool online deal where your book is offered for free to 5 million eager readers. You've heard stories where other writers did this and ended up selling 50,000 copies of their book. It costs you $350. 400 people download your book for free. The resulting bump in paid sales never happens.

This goes on endlessly until you realize that you are bleeding money and so you stop marketing your book. Your sales go to zero.

THE WAY FORWARD:

Learn from your mistakes. Write a business plan and stick to it, or start thinking of what you are doing as a hobby and make peace with what it costs.

"There's no money in poetry, but then there's no poetry in money either."
— Robert Graves

SECTION NINE

The Agonies of Bad Timing

35.

ANOTHER WRITER WRITES YOUR BOOK, BUT WRITES IT BETTER THAN YOU DO

You write a book about how technology is robbing our children of creativity. It's a pretty good book. It gets some attention, and you make some sales. Momentum seems to be building — and then, a few weeks later, another book is released about how technology is robbing our children of creativity. It has a catchier title. It has a jazzier cover. The author is great on TV. *The Times* gives him a front-of-the-book-review review, and The Today Show has him on at the top of the hour. Suddenly, he's everywhere. You see him quoted in the *Washington Post*. His book is excerpted in *The Wall Street Journal*. There's a feature store in *People*. You are so furious that, on your way home from storming to the store to buy chocolate chip cookie dough, you back your car into a fire hydrant. You are so angry that, when the cops arrive to take a statement, you swear at them. They threaten to cuff you. When you back down, they tell you to go home and take it easy.

But you don't. You can't. You hatch plans to hunt the other author down. You actually look up his address on Zillow. You stalk him on Facebook. You scroll through his website looking for evidence that he somehow stole your idea, but he didn't; his credentials are solid. So you punch his face, which is to say you punch your computer screen, and end up waiting seven hours to get into the emergency room for stitches. Your hand is so badly cut, you can't write for three months, which is all for the best, because no one is asking for your second book.

THE WAY FORWARD:

Calm down, take a deep breath, and think about what you will write next.

"Resentment is like drinking poison and waiting for the other person to die."
— Carrie Fisher

36.

YOUR BOOK LAUNCH IS UPSTAGED BY SOME UNPREDICTABLE HEADLINE-GRABBING NATIONAL STORY

You've got book signings planned, an interview at the big local TV station in each town on your tour, and VIPs event at every stop. You have so many appearances, in fact, that you have an appointment to get your nails done. You're on your way, when you hear it on the radio: Big bad news. You listen, first, as a citizen. Oh no. You listen second, as a family member: is everyone in your family okay? You listen third as an author. But what about my book signing? What about my interview? What about my VIP event? All of them are cancelled. For the next four weeks, the only news will be about this big thing that's happened, and by the time the nation is back on the way to recovery, your book is a thing of the past.

THE WAY FORWARD:

Calm down, take a deep breath, put the experience into perspective, and think about what you will write next.

"I wish I had known that publishing a novel is a crapshoot from start to finish... Don't take it

personally. That's the best advice for a writer, the key to an even-keel sanity with regard to the whole business—don't take anything personally."

—Kate Christensen

37.

YOU BECOME SO JEALOUS OF YOUR WRITER FRIENDS THAT YOU CAN'T SEE STRAIGHT

You have a writer pal who has been working on her book for approximately the same number of years that you have been working on your book. When you are having a bad day, or can't see your way out of a thorny story problem, you call her and she gets it, as much as anyone is likely to get it. She makes you laugh, urges you on, and you love her for this. You try to offer her the same support on her bad days. You treasure this working relationship. You consider this friend your writing North Star. One fine day, your friend calls in a burst of joy. She has sold her book for a fat chunk of change. You scream with delight, rush over with roses and champagne and savor the goodness of a good person getting a bit of good luck. Not long afterwards, you sell your book and she returns the favor of the flowers and the champagne, and you laugh at the fact that it is, indeed, an abundant universe. There is room for both your books. There are enough readers for every story.

Soon, however, your paths begin to diverge. Your friend's book gets picked for the Barnes & Noble Discovery New Voices program — and yours does not. Your friend's book gets selected to appear in a summer promotion for Target — and yours does not. Your friend is invited to speak at Book Expo America — and you are not. Her book hits the bestseller list — and yours does not.

You try to remember how abundant the universe is and you try to be happy for her, but it becomes more and more difficult. You have to stop going on Facebook, where her readers gush. You have to stop reading your favorite blogs, where her book is being featured in reviews and advertisements. You can't even go into your favorite local bookstore, because her book is stacked on the front table with a lovely handwritten shelf talker note from a staff member beside it, and yours sits alone on a shelf somewhere in the back of the store, near the floorboards, hidden by a spinning rack of greeting cards.

She sells another book — and you don't. You want to be happy for her, but your happiness is clearly strained. She knows it. You know it. And so you stop calling her — the one person who could most help you get over your jealousy, the one person whose good fortune you could most truly understand.

THE WAY FORWARD:

Writing a book is a long, hard, difficult, lonely undertaking. Why do it if you don't care about it with a fiery passion? It would be far easier and more pleasant to grow heirloom tomatoes or take up paddle boarding. Jealousy proves that you're nowhere near ready to throw in the towel. Oh sure, you may go through weeks or months of claiming that you are going to quit writing, of claiming that it is just too painful, of claiming that you are done with this fickle business where you can pour out your heart and soul and get nothing but silence in return. But you aren't fooling anyone, least of all yourself. In *The Happiness Project*, Gretchen Ruben says that failure is "part of being ambitious; it's part of being creative." Jealous, too. So if you're feeling jealousy of another writer, consider it a good thing. It means you've found something that matters to you. Feel it, and then forget it and go back to doing that thing.

"You know what I do when I feel jealous? I tell myself to not feel jealous. I shut down the why not me? voice and replace it with one that says don't be silly instead. It really is that easy. You actually do stop being an awful jealous person by stopping being an awful jealous person. When you feel like crap because someone has gotten something you want you force yourself to remember how very much you have been given. You remember that there is plenty for all of us. You remember that someone else's success has absolutely no bearing on your own. You remember that a wonderful thing has happened to one of your literary peers and maybe, if you keep working and if you get lucky, something wonderful may also someday happen to you."

— *Cheryl Strayed,* writing as Dear Sugar.

SECTION TEN

The Agonies of Going Public

38.

THE REVIEWERS RIP YOU TO SHREDS

They call you names, disparage your work, mock your efforts. Reading their reviews takes you straight back to that time in kindergarten when you stood in front of the class to give a report on butterflies and got so nervous you peed in your pants. Same humiliation. Same gut-wrenching shame. Back then, you pulled the covers over your head and refused to go to school the next day. Now you pull the covers over your head and refuse to leave the house. In forty-seven years, you have made no progress.

THE WAY FORWARD:

The best thing to do is to (privately) hate the reviewers right back, and then forget what they said and keep writing.

"An absolutely necessary part of a writer's equipment, almost as necessary as talent, is the ability to stand up under punishment, both the punishment the world hands out and the punishment he inflicts upon himself."
— Irwin Shaw

39.

YOU HOLD A BOOK SIGNING AND NO ONE COMES

Your publicist arranged a book signing at Sweet Neighborhood Bookstore, in a town about an hour from where you live. You don't know anyone in this town, so you drive down early and grab dinner at the Whole Foods deli. You find the bookstore, and then drive around the block a few times looking for parking. When you find a spot, you walk back to the store and stand on the sidewalk out front gazing at the stacks of your books in the window and at the giant poster of your book cover. Someone has made a sign that says, "Author reading tonight!" You take a picture, making sure to include in the frame the stacks of John Irving's latest novel, the stacks of Malcolm Gladwell's latest treatise on the way we behave, and the stacks of the Barefoot Contessa's new cookbook. You have never felt more awesome in your entire life. You feel that you know, now, the true meaning of success and contentment. You have done it! You have written a book!

A slightly disheveled woman walks by with a dog on a leash. The dog stops to sniff by the window, and it sniffs your shoe and so you smile at the woman, nod at the window, and say, "I'm the author." The woman smiles. "Congratulations," she says. You smile back. "Thank you so much." The woman yanks her dog away and continues on her path, so you go into the store.

The young man at the counter looks up and says your name. He recognizes you from your author photo. He directs you to the stack of books set out on the table and hands you a Sharpie. "We'd like you to sign a dozen for the store," he says. You see that he is making out a shelf talker that says, "Signed copies available!" You sit and sign the books and chat with the counter guy about traffic and the weather and the new John Irving novel. There are half a dozen customers in the store, browsing and reading and making their way quietly through the stacks. There's another bookstore employee who wanders in and out, asking if you'd like water or tea. She's the first one to look at her watch. She's the first one to speak about what is happening, or rather what is not happening. "People often come late on Thursdays," she says, "It can be a busy night." You smile and chat with her about the Barefoot Contessa's roasted tomato soup recipe, which you recently had at a potluck.

Counter Guy makes an announcement. "Our author reading will begin in five minutes," he calls out, hoping to summon the customers to fill at least a few of the black folding chairs set up before you. There are 27 chairs. You know because you counted them. None of the customers emerge.

The bell on the door tinkles and you look up with huge hope, only to see a mother dragging two small girls, and talking loudly about not touching any of the stuffed animals. They have come to pick up a birthday present for a party. You surmise this because one of the little girls has on sparkly red shoes and the other has on sparkly pink. Watch Girl steps in to help them, and you watch the small drama unfold – the choosing of the gift, the wrapping of it, the paying.

When the party-goers are gone, Watch Girl looks at her watch again and then turns to you. "Let's give it five more minutes."

You nod and get up and go look at the shelf of poetry behind the rows of empty chairs. After five minutes, Counter Guy comes out from behind the counter and folds himself into one of the folding chairs. "You can read to us," he says, "It will be good practice, anyway."

"Sure!" you say, as if you were just offered an all-expenses paid trip to the moon. As Watch Girl perches next to Counter Guy, you launch into the program you prepared — a few comments about your background and how you came to write the book, and then you pick up your book, turn to the page you carefully marked with a Post-It, and read the words you slaved over. As you read, you want to die. You are amazed that you can have such a strong, clear intention separate from the actions of your mind and your mouth. You are reading your book out loud in a bookstore, and yet you want nothing more than to die.

When you are finished reading, you close the book and Counter Guy and Watch Girl clap enthusiastically. Counter Guy leaps up to help a customer who has made his way to the counter. "Bravo," Watch Girl says, and then she gets up and starts to put away the chairs.

You help her, because what else are you going to do?

THE WAY FORWARD:

Grin and bear it, then go back and read all those posts about platform building that you ignored the first time.

"It takes a lot of time to be a genius. You have to sit around so much, doing nothing, really doing nothing."
— Gertrude Stein

40.

YOU HOLD A BOOK SIGNING TO WHICH HUNDREDS OF EAGER FANS COME, AND YOU REALIZE THAT THEY WON'T BE SATISFIED UNTIL THEY OWN A PIECE OF YOUR SOUL

Your publicist arranged a book signing at Sweet Neighborhood Bookstore, in a town about an hour from where you live. You don't know anyone in this town, so you drive down early and grab dinner at the Whole Foods deli. You find the bookstore and then drive around the block a few times looking for parking. When you find a spot, you walk back to the store and stand on the sidewalk out front gazing at the stacks of your book in the window and at the giant poster of your book cover. You don't even have time to take a picture, before a young man bursts out of the bookstore and calls your name. "We're so glad you're here," he says, "There have been customers lining up for an hour. We're already sold 30 copies! We had to put out more chairs!"

You follow him inside and the place is packed! It is buzzing. Readers rush up to ask you to sign their books, and so you sit at a table and another bookstore employee — a girl with red hair and a funky red watch — stands next to you asking customers to spell their names. She writes these names on a Post-It note, which she slaps on the cover so that when the readers get to you, you don't have to ask them how to spell their name. You chat with each reader about their experience with your book, and their lives, and you are amazed at how instantly intimate people are with you. It's almost as if the readers are coming to confession and you are the priest who can absolve them of their sins. It's almost as if you are Oprah, sitting on the couch.

It's somewhat disconcerting, at first, but you warm up to it. Soon you realize that you have never felt more awesome in your entire life. You feel that you know, now, the true meaning of success and contentment. You have done it! You have written a book! And people like it! They really like it! After about fifteen minutes, Counter Guy announces that the reading is going to start now, and asks people to please take their seats. Watch Girl asks if you'd like a cup of tea.

You say a few comments about your background and how you came to write the book, and then you pick up your book, turn to the page you carefully marked with a Post-It, and start to read. The audience laughs. They guffaw. They sit in rapt silence. It is awesome. When you are finished, and the applause has died down, you ask if there are any questions. One woman in the first row, whose name you remember was Juliee, with two e's, raises her hand.

"The scene when the mother tries to fix her daughter's painting was outstanding. It was my favorite part of the book. I loved it. I wondered how you thought to write a scene like that, with a mother who is such a monster. You would never dare do that to your child's art, would you?"

The truth is that you did do it, once, when your daughter was in third grade. It wasn't in an art gallery and it wasn't a prized painting, but still, you did it. You are that monster. You look out at the crowd and they look hungry – as if they will eat you up. You want to guard this one piece of yourself, this small bit of your life. "No of course not," you say, "But I have certainly thought about it. I tried to put myself in the shoes of a woman who would dare."

The crowd nods, satisfied, and another hand shoots up. “The scene where the lifeguard sucks on Lily’s toes was so sexy,” this woman says, “but I’ve never even thought of doing that. I’ve never imagined it. You and your husband do that, do you? I mean, have you *done* that?”

You swallow. Holy crap! You can’t believe a stranger actually asked you this question in public. You can’t believe she cares. You can’t believe you have to answer. “I’m not going to give away all my secrets,” you say coyly, and everyone laughs, but you understand now that these people are vultures. They will pick every scrap of flesh from your body if you let them.

THE WAY FORWARD:

Count your blessings and think with compassion of George Clooney and Beyonce.

Or become one of those writers who never leaves the house and refuses to give interviews.

“Fifty Shades of Grey is a fantasy -- have they forgotten what that means? Do they chase J.K. Rowling down the street daring her to use her Avada Kedavra spell? Do they ask Hilary Mantel how many courtiers she's beheaded?"
— Niall Leonard, husband of mega-bestselling Fifty Shades trilogy author E.L. James

41.

YOU GET HATE MAIL

You have been getting a lot of fan mail lately, and it has become a favorite part of your day. You love to open the notes and hear what your readers think of your book -- how it moved them and entertained them. Many readers ask when your next book is coming out and you write them back and say, "Soon!" You can write faster, knowing there are such kind people out there waiting for your book.

One day, you open a note and start reading. "I loved the start of the story and the whole premise and set up," the reader says, "but I soon found myself yelling at you, and ended up throwing the book across the room." *That seems rather violent,* you think, and you take a deep breath and keep reading.

"Anyone who can imagine a character who hates dogs is not worthy of my time," the reader says. "So I threw your book away. I left it in the garbage at the airport. I have never thrown a book away before, and I wanted to let you know that yours was the first. You should be ashamed of yourself."

You take another deep breath and begin to write this reader back. You spend three hours crafting a carefully worded response, and then delete it. You spend two more hours writing an angry attack that talks about freedom of expression and the philosophy of fiction, and then delete it. You call your writer friends and ask for their advice. You don't sleep for days, wondering about this person, and wondering if maybe she is right: you should be ashamed.

You finally write her back a short, whiny little note saying you are sorry she was disappointed. Three months later, you can recite her note word for word, and each of your responses — the one you sent and the ones you didn't send. You cannot remember a single specific positive thing that anyone ever said about the book.

THE WAY FORWARD:

A book is like a stone dropped into a pond. Sometimes the ripples are going to be fabulous, positive, soul-enriching praise. Sometimes the ripples are going to sound like the whispering of the devil himself. Remember that hearing negative feedback is better than hearing nothing at all.

Once you've grasped that idea, try to imagine what a flat, dry, sad little life the writer of the nasty letter is living. Try to imagine that she does not know the thunderous joy and satisfaction of making something — only the pale pleasure of using her free time to point fingers at other people's creations. Picture her with a mean, smelly old dog who throws up on the rug every night.

"It's easy to attack and destroy an act of creation. It's a lot more difficult to perform one."
— Chuck Palahniuk

SECTION ELEVEN

The Agony of the Numbers

42.

YOU DON'T EARN OUT YOUR ADVANCE

A publisher gives you a healthy advance for your book. You get a check on signing, and another check when you turn in the manuscript. When the book launches it sells briskly for a few months, but it does not make any bestseller lists, it is not chosen as a perfect summer read by a national women's magazine, and it is not picked up by Costco. One day, you go onto amazon.com and you see that your book has been deeply discounted. A few months later, you find that it can be purchased for a penny. For the next five years, your agent sends you royalty reports with negative numbers. Your book sold, but it did not sell enough to earn any royalties.

Building a writing career is a long game, you tell yourself. *I'm in it for the long haul.* So you write another book. It's your best work yet, and your agent takes it out with great fanfare. Editors respond with huge enthusiasm. They love it! They take it to their pub boards. And then one by one, the editors come back to your agent with this news: the numbers on your last book aren't good enough. The numbers make them nervous. If it weren't for the numbers on the last book, they would have loved to publish your new book.

THE WAY FORWARD:

Cry, and consider taking a pen name.

"Writing isn't about making money, getting famous, getting dates, getting laid, or making friends. In the end, it's about enriching the lives of those who will read your work, and enriching your own life, as well. It's about getting up, getting well, and getting over. Getting happy, okay? Getting happy."

— Stephen King

SECTION TWELVE

The Agonies of Wanting to do it Again

43.

AGAINST YOUR BETTER JUDGMENT, YOU HAVE AN IDEA FOR ANOTHER BOOK

You're in the shower, soaping up your hair. You have a million things to do that day — when out of the blue, wholly unbidden, an idea for another book hits you like a bolt of lightning. You know exactly how much it is going to cost you to write this book — how much time, how much energy, how much despair — and you wish with all your heart that you could pretend you never had the idea, but you had it. It now owns you.

THE WAY FORWARD:

Just write it.

"You are lucky to be one of those people who wishes to build sand castles with words, who is willing to create a place where your imagination can wander. We build this place with the sand of memories; these castles are our memories and inventiveness made tangible. So part of us believes that when the tide starts coming in, we won't really have lost anything, because actually only a symbol of it was there in the sand. Another part of us thinks we'll figure out a way

to divert the ocean. This is what separates artists from ordinary people: the belief, deep in our hearts, that if we build our castles well enough, somehow the ocean won't wash them away. I think this is a wonderful kind of person to be."

— Anne Lamott

ABOUT THE AUTHOR

My name is Jennie Nash. I'm the author of seven books — three memoirs, four novels, and counting. I have been on staff at Random House and *New York Woman* magazine, and have freelanced for dozens of publications, including *GQ, Child, Glamour, The Huffington Post,* and *The New York Times.* I am an instructor at the UCLA Extension Writer's Program, and run a private practice coaching both fiction and non-fiction book writers. I am also the Chief Creative Officer and developer of the **Author Accelerator** program (www.authoraccelerator.com), which gives writers weekly lessons, feedback, and accountability so they can finally finish their books.

FREE STUFF!

Go to www.jennienash.com and sign up for my free Friday newsletter. I teach key lessons about writing and the writing life each week – and when you sign up, you'll get a downloadable copy of **The No Excuses Book Map**, which lays out the entire process of writing and publishing a book.

Wondering if the Author Accelerator might be right for you? Write to Matt@authoraccelerator.com with **"Writers' Guide Free Trial"** in the subject line. We'll sign you up for a free trial of The Author Accelerator, which includes a video lesson, daily emails, and a personalized, professional edit of 10 pages.

www.ingramcontent.com/pod-product-compliance
Lightning Source LLC
Chambersburg PA
CBHW070358290526
45790CB00004B/1541

9781507862117